SMALLEST ANIMALS

ANIMALS

That's Wild!
A Look at Animals

Julie Murray

Big Buddy BOOKS
That's Wild!

ABDO
Publishing Company

VISIT US AT
www.abdopublishing.com

Published by ABDO Publishing Company, 8000 West 78th Street, Edina, Minnesota 55439.

Printed in the United States of America, North Mankato, Minnesota.
112009
012010

 PRINTED ON RECYCLED PAPER

Coordinating Series Editor: Rochelle Baltzer
Editor: Sarah Tieck
Contributing Editors: Heidi M.D. Elston, Megan M. Gunderson, BreAnn Rumsch, Marcia Zappa
Graphic Design: Deborah Coldiron, Maria Hosley
Cover Photographs: *Eighth Street Studio*; *Fotosearch*: Asia Images, RF; *iStockphoto*: ©iStockphoto.com/Rouzes.
Interior Photographs/Illustrations: *AP Photo*: Kelly Gillin/The Wenatchee World/File (p. 29); *Cal Photos*: Alessandro Catenazzi (p. 19), Pierre Fidenci (p. 5), Ansel Fong (p. 17); *Corbis*: ©Steven Kazlowski/Science Faction (p. 21); *Eighth Street Studio* (pp. 14, 20, 25, 30); Copyright S. Blair Hedges/Penn State (p. 15); *iStockphoto*: ©iStockphoto.com/cveltri (p. 23), ©iStockphoto.com/Derrical (p. 23), ©iStockphoto.com/Kirham (p. 8), ©iStockphoto.com/mammamaart (p. 29), ©iStockphoto.com/John Pitcher (p. 29), ©iStockphoto.com/Saphra (p. 7), ©iStockphoto.com/Hugh Stonelan (p. 8), ©iStockphoto.com/stray_cat (p. 19); *Minden Pictures*: Mark Moffett (p. 17); *Peter Arnold, Inc.*: ©Biosphoto/Gunther Michel (p. 11), Reinhard, H./Arco Images (p. 11); *Photo Researchers, Inc.*: ©Dr. Merlin D. Tuttle (p. 26), ©Dr. Merlin D. Tuttle/Bat Conservation International (p. 5); Jim Sanderson (p. 13); Joel Sartore (p. 5); *Shutterstock*: Henrik Andersen (p. 15), Anette (p. 7), Natalia D. (p. 15), Karel Gallas (p. 25), Lasse Kristensen (p. 29), Michael Lynch (pp. 5, 23), Marek Slusarczyk (p. 21), André Viegas (p. 13), Nicole Weiss (p. 7), Vladimir Wrangel (p. 11) .

Library of Congress Cataloging-in-Publication Data

Murray, Julie, 1969-
  Smallest animals / Julie Murray.
    p. cm. -- (That's wild! : a look at animals)
  ISBN 978-1-60453-980-6
  1. Body size--Juvenile literature. I. Title.
  QL799.3.M873 2010
  590--dc22
                          2009033008

Contents

Wildly Small!

Pygmy Rabbit

Many amazing animals live in our world. Some are fast and others are slow. They may fly, run, or swim.

Some animals are wildly small! Their size can help them survive in their **habitats**. Being small might help them hide from predators or move without being noticed. Let's learn more about small animals!

Pacific Ocean

Monte Iberia Eleuth

4

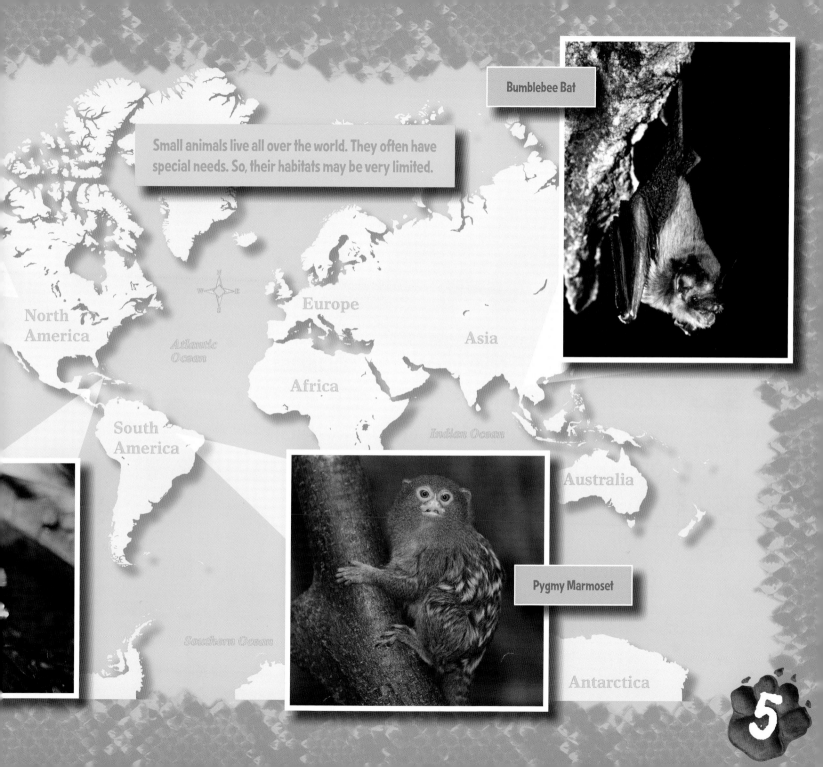

Small animals live all over the world. They often have special needs. So, their habitats may be very limited.

Bumblebee Bat

Pygmy Marmoset

North America

Europe

Asia

Atlantic Ocean

Africa

South America

Indian Ocean

Australia

Southern Ocean

Antarctica

5

Bow Wow

The Chihuahua is the world's smallest type of dog. Chihuahuas have very short legs and slim bodies. Most adults weigh less than six pounds (3 kg)! And, they usually measure less than nine inches (23 cm) tall.

Chihuahuas are so small that they fit easily in purses and bags.

Many Chihuahuas have very short hair (*right*). Those with longer hair (*above*) require more brushing.

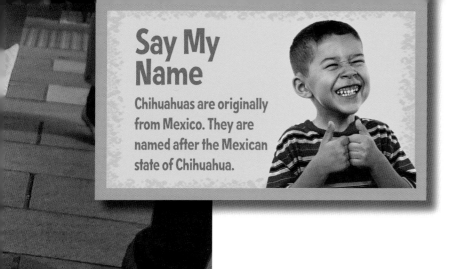

Although they are small, Chihuahuas are known for their big **personalities**. Chihuahuas often **protect** people and property. So, they can make good watchdogs.

Chihuahuas are popular pets. They often appear in movies and on television.

9

Small World

One of the smallest **reptiles** is the Jaragua Sphaero. It is also called a dwarf gecko. This lizard's body is less than one inch (3 cm) long! And, it weighs less than .1 ounces (3 g)!

Scientists first reported their discovery in 2001. There could be other even smaller reptiles in the wild.

Many small lizards are called dwarf geckos. These include the white-headed dwarf gecko (*above*) and the turquoise dwarf gecko (*right*).

When curled up, the Jaragua Sphaero's entire body could fit on a nickel!

11

Here Kitty, Kitty

The kodkod is one of the smallest types of wildcats. It lives in South America.

Kodkods weigh only about four to six pounds (2 to 3 kg). Yet, they are mighty hunters. They eat **rodents**, birds, and bugs. Sometimes, they even steal chickens from farms!

Some kodkods live in the Andes Mountains. They hide away in their forest home.

12

Kodkods are smaller than average house cats.

13

Noodle It

A Barbados threadsnake's body is as thin as a spaghetti noodle!

The Barbados threadsnake is one of the world's smallest snakes. It lives on the **tropical** island of Barbados.

These snakes are just four inches (10 cm) long, and they are blind. These features make them easy for predators to catch. So, they **burrow** into the ground to **protect** themselves.

Islands are often home to unusual animals.

15

Hop To It

There are some very small frogs in the world. Scientists aren't sure which is the smallest. That's because they keep finding smaller ones.

Two of the smallest frogs are the Monte Iberia Eleuth and the Brazilian gold frog. Both measure about .39 inches (10 mm)!

The Monte Iberia Eleuth makes a high-pitched croaking noise. Its voice box is as small as a pinhead!

The Brazilian gold frog is also called Izecksohn's toad.

17

Another small frog is the Noble's pygmy frog. This frog is .43 inches (11 mm) long.

The Noble's pygmy frog lives in the Andes Mountains of South America. Its brownish skin and small size help it hide among trees.

Did You Hear That?

Scientists first found the Noble's pygmy frog because they heard it croaking.

Danger!
When rabbits are scared, they thump their back feet on the ground. This is loud enough to warn nearby rabbits.

Too Cute!

Pygmy rabbits are the smallest rabbits in North America. These tiny bunnies weigh about one pound (.5 kg). They measure about ten inches (25 cm) long.

Pygmy rabbits have short, strong legs and good hearing. These features help keep them safe. The rabbits can also make sounds to communicate with other rabbits.

Pygmy rabbits often hide in sagebrush. Most animals don't eat this plant, but pygmy rabbits do.

21

Monkey Around

Pygmy marmosets are the world's smallest monkeys. These tiny creatures can easily fit in the palm of a person's hand! They weigh between three and seven ounces (85 and 198 g).

A pygmy marmoset's body is about six inches (15 cm) long. Its tail may grow longer than its body. It can measure six to nine inches (15 to 23 cm) long.

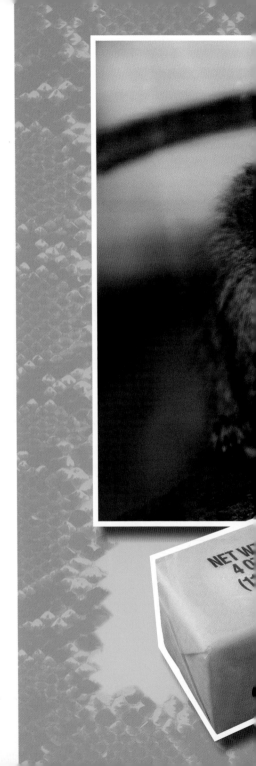

22

The smallest pygmy marmosets weigh less than a stick of butter!

BUTTER NET WT 4 OZ (113g)

BUTTER

23

Pygmy marmosets live in South America's rain forests. These tiny creatures move quickly through the treetops. They stay out of sight of predators, such as birds.

Pygmy marmoset families include two to nine members. They like to live in large spaces. And, they work hard to **protect** this space. Sometimes, they even chase away other animals.

Pygmy marmosets have sharp teeth. They cut through very tough tree bark to get to sap.

Awwww!

Baby pygmy marmosets are often so small they can wrap their bodies around a human finger.

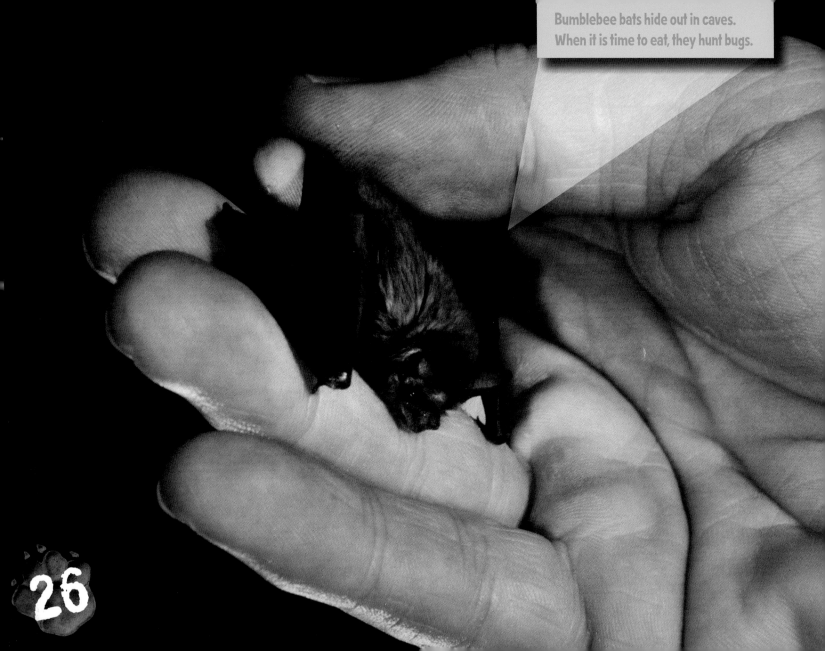

26

Bee Batty

Scientists believe the bumblebee bat is the world's smallest mammal. It lives in Thailand and Myanmar. Even though it is a bat, it is closer to the size of a bumblebee!

These tiny bats weigh less than .1 ounces (3 g). And, their bodies measure about one inch (3 cm) long. With their wings stretched out, bumblebee bats are about six inches (15 cm) wide.

That WAS wild!

From tiny bunnies to noodle-sized snakes, there are some very small wild animals. Each of them is an important part of the animal kingdom.

People work hard to **protect** animals and their surroundings. You can help, too! Recycling and using less water are two simple things you can do. The more you learn, the more you can do to help keep animals safe.

It is important to not waste water. This helps protect the planet.

Observe animal homes from a distance. Humans can harm animal homes by touching them. They may also scare the animal.

Pygmy rabbit populations are threatened. But, scientists and other people are working to save them.

29

Wow! Is That TRUE?

🐾 The smallest bird is the bee hummingbird. It is so tiny it can sit on a pencil eraser!

🐾 The infantfish of Australia is the world's smallest fish. It is less than one-half inch (1 cm) long!

🐾 Some of the smallest reptiles are the Brookesia chameleons. These tiny lizards live on the forest floor in Madagascar. If they feel unsafe, they play dead and try to look like fallen leaves.

Important Words

burrow to dig a tunnel or a hole in the ground.

habitat a place where a living thing is naturally found.

mammal a group of living beings. Mammals have hair and make milk to feed their babies.

personality (puhr-suh-NA-luh-tee) the set of emotions and behaviors that make some creatures different from others.

protect (pruh-TEHKT) to guard against harm or danger.

reptile a group of living beings. Reptiles have scaly skin and are cold blooded.

rodent any of several related animals that have large front teeth for gnawing. Common rodents include mice, squirrels, and beavers.

tropical relating to an area on Earth where it is hot all year.

Web Sites

To learn more about small animals, visit ABDO Publishing Company online. Web sites about small animals are featured on our Book Links page. These links are routinely monitored and updated to provide the most current information available.

www.abdopublishing.com

31

Index